# KAIVALYA NAVANEETA

## THE CREAM OF EMANCIPATION

An Ancient Tamil Classic by Tandavaraya Swami

Translated into English *by*
Swami Sri Ramanananda Saraswathi
(Munagala S. Venkataramaiah)

SRI RAMANASRAMAM
TIRUVANNAMALAI
INDIA

**KAIVALYA NAVANEETA** (English).
Original work in Tamil: *Kaivalya Navaneetam* by Tandavaraya Swami
Translated by Swami Ramanananda Saraswathi
(Munagala S. Venkataramaiah).



*First Edition: 1965; Second Edition: 1974*
*Third Edition: 1981; Fourth Edition: 1993 (2000 copies)*
*Fifth Edition: 1997 (3000 copies); Sixth Edition: 2006 (2000)*
*Seventh Edition: 2011 (1000); Eighth Edition: 2013 (1000 copies)*
*Ninth Edition: 2016; Tenth Edition: 2022 (1000 copies)*
Eleventh Edition: 2024 — (500 copies)
Twelfth Edition: 2025 — 2000 copies

CC No: 1023

ISBN: 978-81-88018-44-4

Price: ₹ 60

*Published by:*
Venkat S. Ramanan
President
SRI RAMANASRAMAM
Tiruvannamalai 606 603.
Tamil Nadu, INDIA
Email : ashram@gururamana.org
Web : www.gururamana.org

*Printed by:*
Sudarsan Graphics Pvt. Ltd.,
Chennai - 600 041

# PUBLISHER'S NOTE

We have great pleasure in offering to the devotees of Sri Bhagavan and the students of Vedanta in general, a valuable little classic. This was one of the works very frequently referred to by the Maharshi.

In the absence of any mention in earlier literature on Vedanta in Tamil we can assume that 'Kaivalya Navaneeta' was probably written at least five hundred years ago. It was translated into German and English by Dr. Charles Graul DD of the Leipzig Lutheran Mission and we have in the Ramanasramam Library a book containing these German and English translations and published in 1855, both in Leipzig and London. We have not come across any other English translation so far.

We are confident that this great little book will prove to be of immense help to all sadhaks.

01-09-2006 — SRI RAMANASRAMAM
*Advent Day* — Tiruvannamalai

# INTRODUCTION

*Kaivalya Navaneeta* is a widely known Advaita classic in Tamil. *Navaneeta* means butter. *Kaivalya* or *Kevala* is the state in which the soul exists, isolated from all connection with the body, etc. From the vast ocean of milk (the *Upanishads* etc.) the great teachers have drawn the milk of wisdom and filled it in pots (ancient texts). Tandavaraya Swami, the author of the *Kaivalya Navaneeta* says that he has extracted the butter from the milk. Those who have obtained this (being fed on the butter of divine wisdom — *Brahma jnana* — and being eternally satisfied) will not roam about feeding on dust (non-real objects of sense).

Verses 175 and 179 contain references to Narayana Desikar of Nannilam, as the preceptor of the author of this work. The author extols the greatness of his parents who had the prophetic insight to give him an appropriate name. Tandava is interpreted in the present context as one who was beckoned to leap across the sea of births as well as one who dances eternally in the delight resulting from divine wisdom.

The two sections of this work are called 'The exposition of the Truth' (*Tattva vilakkappadalam*) and 'Doubts cleared Away' (*Sandeham telitarppadalam*). They explain the basic philosophical principles and clear doubts which are likely to arise in understanding these principles.

In language easy to understand, the author gives a remarkably clear exposition of the tenets of advaita. Its

English translation will serve to make it known to a larger circle of readers and thus extend its usefulness.

University of Madras, V. A. DEVASENAPATHI,
19th July, 1965. Professor of Philosophy.

Bhagavan Sri Ramana Maharshi
(1879 - 1950)

Thou dost root out the ego of those who meditate on Thee in the Heart, Oh Arunachala!
— *Arunachala Aksharamanamalai*, v. 1

# KAIVALYA NAVANEETA

## THE CREAM OF EMANCIPATION

1. Prostrations to the Holy Feet of the Unique Lord who like ether remains as sole witness in the hearts of all beings, whether they are swayed by desire for wealth, lands, and women, or are free from such desire, and who shines as the towering peak over the seven successive spiritual heights,[1] which are in themselves exalted over all other planes (of mind), or in Nannilam, the holiest of the seven holy places!

2. I worship ever-shining Pure Consciousness, which manifests as Brahma, Vishnu, or Mighty Shiva, according as He creates, preserves or withdraws (the universe), and also as the countless individual beings; yet It remains ever-free and perfect, as the blazing sun over the ocean of Bliss.

3. Always I worship the lotus feet of my Master by whose grace I learnt that my very self is the all embracing Reality (Brahman) — and that the mosaic of the universe is but a phenomenon in me — and who remained as the Self, like the ether in a wall.

4. I adore the Almighty who manifested as my Master in order that the mind, the intellect, the senses and the body, might to my very knowledge be reduced to nothing,

---

[1] See Section II, verse 149, and Appendix I.

like mist before the sun, when He taught me "You and I are one," so to make me one with Him!

5. I adore the feet of the holy Master who shines forth for ever as the wide Expanse, which has no beginning or end or interval, and I proceed to tell you the true nature of the Absolute Being, to explain bondage and liberation, so that even those who are too dull to learn the scriptures, may understand.

6. All the ancient sages drew from the boundless ocean of milk, namely the Vedanta,[2] and filled their pitchers, their works.[3] I boiled them all (on the fire of the Master's words), churned them (with the churn of enquiry into the self) and I present this cream of Emancipation — *Kaivalya Navaneeta* — to all.

Now, will those who have partaken of this and satisfied their hunger, roam about eating the offal of externals?[4]

7. After adoring my Master, Venkatesa Mukunda, who is himself ever-free, and who made me his own, I write this *Kaivalya Navaneeta,* divided into two parts, the first of which contains a clear exposition of the Truth,[5] and the second clears away all doubts arising from the former.[6]

---

[2] The *Upanishads.*

[3] The *sutras*, the *itihasas*, the *kavyas* and *bhashyas.*

[4] *i.e.*, seek fulfilment of their desire for worldly life.

[5] *Tattva-vilakkam.*

[6] *Sandehantelithal.*

THE FIRST SECTION

# THE EXPOSITION OF THE TRUTH

8. The Sages say that there are four prerequisites[1] for realisation of the Truth: (1) *Viveka*: discrimination between the temporary (therefore unreal phenomena) and the permanent (therefore the Reality, *i.e.*, the noumenal); (2) indifference to the enjoyment of pleasures here or hereafter; (3) the group of six qualities and (4) the longing for Liberation.

9 & 10. The six qualities are *sama, dama, uparati, titiksha, samadhana* and *sraddha*. Of these, *sama* is control of mind; *dama* is control of the senses; *uparati* is cessation of activities (relating to caste, creed, family, etc.); *titiksha* is control of passions, and includes endurance; *samadhana* is, according to the sages, the settling down of the mind to reflect on the Truth, as revealed (by the scriptures and the sages); *sraddha* denotes faith in the Master and the scriptures. Such are the meanings of the six terms of this category.

11. No one can achieve anything in the world without being properly equipped for the task. For the same reason, only those who are equipped with these four categories of prerequisites can gain illumination. A novice cannot get it so readily. If so gained, it follows that the person has been successively purified in countless incarnations in the past.

---

[1] *Sadhanas*.

12. He alone is fit for knowledge who, suffering from the three kinds of troubles rising from the self, the elements, and Providence (from hunger, thirst and so forth; from heat, cold, rain, disease, and the like; from robbers, wild animals, etc.), squirmed like a worm scorched by heat and panted for a dip in the nectar of wisdom, so as to put an end to the series of rebirths.

13. As the desire for Liberation grew, he became unconcerned about his wife, children and property, ran away from them like an antelope which had extricated itself from the noose of a hunter, sought a holy Master and respected him with all his heart.

14. After eagerly saluting his Master, he stood up and sobbed out his heart, saying, "O Lord! I have suffered long the torture of worldly life, which is after all so false! Gracious Master, save me by tearing off the cords which bind me to the five sheaths, so that my heart may be at peace!"

15. The Master lovingly considered him, like a tortoise its eggs; looked at him, like a fish its eggs; and passed his hands over him, like a bird its wings over its eggs, and said, "There is a means to put an end to your rebirths. I will tell you, and if you act upon it your rebirths will cease."[2]

16. At the very sound of the words "Your rebirths will cease," his frame thrilling, his heart rejoicing as if refreshed after a bath in a spacious tank, tears of joy flowing, like love welling forth, he held the holy feet of the Master and prayed further:

---

[2] This symbolises the three kinds of initiation — by thought, by look and by touch.

17. "Even if I, your servant, am unable to carry out your instructions, you can set me right by your grace. You said just now: "There is a means to put an end to your rebirths! Kindly tell it to me and save me, I pray."

18. Finding him self-subdued, the Master looks at the soul of the disciple, and begins to instruct him, so that it may regain its true nature, as a wasp places a well-chosen caterpillar in its cell of earth, and then buzzes before it.[3]

19 & 20. "Look here, my son! He who has forgotten his true nature is alternately born and dies, turning round and round in the unceasing wheel of time, like a feather caught up in a whirlwind, until he realises the true nature of the Self. If he comes to see the individual self and its substratum, the Overself, then he becomes the substratum, *i.e.*, Brahman, and escapes rebirths. Should you know yourself no harm will befall you. As you asked I have told you this."

*NOTE:* The teaching is complete at this point, and indeed in this verse.

21. *Disciple:* "Lord, do you take me for a fool that you tell me so? Can there be any in the world who are ignorant of the self? How then are they all caught up in the cycle of births and deaths? Tell me the unerring Truth for I beseech you in full faith."

22. *Master:* "Only he is Self-realised who knows what is body and who is embodied."

*Disciple:* "Who else is embodied but this gross thing?" On this, the Master smiled in pity, and spoke:

---

[3] The change of tense is in the original text.

23. "You say that you cannot find the embodied being as different from the gross body. Then tell me who appeared as the subject in your dream; or who experienced the sleep in which even the pain of dream was absent; or again, what is this consciousness in the waking state?"

24. *Disciple:* "Everyday experience proves that the experiencer in the waking state, or the experiencer of the dreams when the waking consciousness is gone, or the experiencer of deep slumber, must be different (from the gross body). Yet it is not realised. It just flashes in the mind, only to fade away at once. Please explain this."

25. Just as people pointing to a tree on the earth to direct the onlooker to the third-day crescent moon (in the sky), and pointing to other stars locate Arundhati (a constellation), so also the sage began pointing to the gross in order to make known the subtle cause.

26. *Master:* "The Vedanta, as a whole, mentions as the cause of bondage and release, superimposition[4] and its effacement,[5] respectively. Bondage is caused by superimposition; release by its effacement.

Now listen as regards the former.

27. Superimposition is seeing one thing in another: a snake, for instance, in a rope; a man in a post; water in mirage; or a blue canopy in the empty sky.

28. Similarly, the five elements and their combinations seen in Brahman, which is free from name and form, one and the same without a second, self-conscious and perfect, are products of illusion.

---

[4] *Aropa*: erroneous knowledge, false attribution, or illusion.

[5] *Apavada*.

29. If you ask how superimposition gives rise to creation (the answer is:)

The beginningless[6] *jivas* remain unmanifest in *avyakta,* as in deep slumber. This state (is disturbed) by the generative thought of *Ishwara* otherwise called Time. Then *avyakta* ceases to be causal (*i.e.* latent) and the three *gunas* manifest.

30. They are *sattva, rajas* and *tamas*, which are pure white, red, and black respectively, or again, clear, turbid and dark. Though equal, one of them will always predominate.

31. This is one explanation. Another is as follows:

The causal state which remains unmanifest, later expands as *mahat tatva* (the totality of the *jivas*), which manifests as the ego, wherein the three *gunas* become apparent.

32. Ether-like *chit* is reflected in them. Of the three *sattva* is clear, and is called *maya*. Brahman reflected in this is *Ishwara*, the intelligent cause of the universe, immanent in all, untainted by *maya* or by any of the *gunas*.

33. This *maya* is the state of deep slumber, the causal body, and the blissful sheath of *Ishwara*. *Rajoguna* is *avidya* (absence of real knowledge). *Chit* reflected in this *guna* (which is not clear owing to its constant agitation), gives rise to countless beings. The *jiva* in this state is known as *prajna*.

34. This is the blissful sheath, the state of deep sleep, and the causal body of the *jivas*. I have so far described the causal stage of superimposition.

Hear me now explain its subtle phase.

---

[6] Whose beginning cannot be known.

35. To provide the wherewithal of experience to the *jivas,* by the loving grace of *Ishwara,* who has all the wondrous powers of His inseparable *maya*, the *tamoguna* then divides itself into its two aspects, namely (1) dense veiling of Reality[7] and (2) multiplicity of phenomena.[8]

36. In the latter of these two, there appears ether; from ether, air; from air, fire; from fire, water; from water, earth. All these five, in the nascent state, are called elements. From these arise bodies suitable for experiences.

37. The three gunas permeate all these five elements. In *sattva*, which is pure, there arise the *jnanendriyas*,[9] of individual function, and also the mind and intellect, of collective function. These seven products of *sattva* form the instruments of knowledge.

38. Then in *rajoguna* there arise the vital airs,[10] of collective function, and the *karmendriyas*,[11] of individual function. These seventeen[12] fundamentals form the subtle bodies of gods, demons, human beings, animals, and all other living organisms.

39. The *jiva*, united to such a body, is called *taijasa*; and *Ishwara*, under similar conditions, is known as *Hiranyagarbha*. In both cases it is called the *linga sharira* or the subtle body which comprises the three sheaths (the vital the mental and the intellectual). This is their dream-state.

---

[7] *Avarana*.

[8] *Vikshepa*.

[9] The senses of hearing, sight, touch, taste and smell.

[10] *Prana, apana, vyana, udana* and *samana*.

[11] Hands, feet, organs of speech, of excretion and of reproduction.

[12] The ten principles mentioned here and the seven contained in the previous stanza.

40. So much for the subtle body. Now hear me describe the process of superimposition of the gross body.

*Ishwara*, who is ever watchful, combined the five elements so as to evolve gross bodies for the *jivas*, and objects for experience.

41. Each of the five elements was divided into two halves; each half was subdivided into four quarters. Then the major half of one element was combined with one quarter subdivision of each of the other four. This process gave rise to the gross elements from which the four classes of beings,[13] and their experiences, the universe and its worlds, were created.

42. The *jiva* united with the gross body, is called *viswa*; and *Ishwara* under similar conditions, is known as *Virat*. The gross body is the physical sheath,[14] and their waking state.

Remember this brief statement regarding the gross body."

43. *Disciple:* "Master! if these states[15] be common to both, how shall we know the difference between exalted *Ishwara* and the ordinary *jiva*?"

*Master:* "The *jiva* is the effect and *Ishwara* the cause. There is also a difference as between units and their totality.

44. The trees form the units; their aggregate is the forest. Generally speaking the mobile and immobile *jivas* are the separate units; their sum total is *Ishwara*. This is the difference between *Ishwara* and the *jivas*.

---

[13] (1) Foetus-born, (2) egg-born, (3) larva-born, and (4) seed-born.

[14] *Annamaya-kosha*, among the *pancha koshas*.

[15] The gross, subtle and causal states which form the *uphadis*.

45. I have said thus far what superimposition is. Only he is a *Jnani* who knows beyond doubt that all that is seen is only ephemeral like a dream.

Now, listen to the process of effacement of superimposition, the way to wonderful *moksha*[16] which resembles the placid sky when all the clouds of winter clear away.

46. (Just as one examines and finds out that) this is not a snake but a rope, and this is not a thief but a thick post, so also one makes out beyond doubt, by the word of the Master and the light of the scriptures, that the body, the world and the elements are only Brahman, *i.e.*, unchanging consciousness.

Know this to be the effacement of superimposition.

47. Cause and effect are the same, like cloth and yarn, ornaments and gold, utensils and clay. To resolve the body into its *antecedent cause*, until *avidya* is traced as the root-cause of all, is the method of effacing superimposition."

48. *Disciple:* "You have said that the *tamoguna* functions in two aspects, namely veiling and multiplicity. You have explained that the latter springs from desire.

Tell me, my Lord, the result of the other aspect — veiling."

49. *Master:* "*Avarana*[17] veils the inner vision of all embodied beings except unexcelled *Ishwara* and Self-realised *Jnanis*, in the shape of 'It is not – It does not shine forth', in the same way as the dense darkness of a wintry night hides the sky, the earth and the directions from our view.

---

[16] Liberation.

[17] *i.e.*, the veiling power.

50. Outwardly this altogether obstructs the distinguishing of Brahman who is Perfection, from His modifications (as the world), and inwardly that of the Self which is pure Consciousness, from Its modifications (as the inner faculties, *i.e.* the ego, the mind). It is therefore the sole cause of that chronic disease, the endless series of births and deaths.

51. The question then arises: Whereon does the superimposition rest when the substratum is completely hidden? And how can there be any superimposition if the substratum is not hidden? (The answer is:) The substratum is twofold, general and particular, of which the general substratum remains continuous and unbroken. Transient superimposition is particular.

52. In the world, the common substratum 'This is' can never be veiled; but only the particular identity — 'This is a rope'. Similarly with the *jiva*, ignorance[18] does not veil the substratum — 'I AM'; but it veils the specific knowledge — 'I am Brahman'."

53. *Disciple:* "How does it happen, my Master, that the power of veiling is censured for the doings of the power of multiplicity which arising as the five sheaths, the *jiva* and the world, obstructs pure Being from view?"

*Master:* "Listen to me, in answer to this question:

54. Although the power of multiplicity is the direct cause of the misery-laden cycle of births (and deaths) yet it is of service

[18] The knowledge 'This is' persists whether we see a rope or a snake. It is unbroken, continuous and general, whereas there is no knowledge of the rope when it is seen as a snake, nor of a snake when it is seen as a rope. Such knowledge is real when the rope is recognised, and unreal when the snake is presumed.

to those who seek Liberation in earnest. Can the darkness of night be of the same service for one's useful activities as the light of day? What more can I say to you? Therefore, my son, the power of veiling is the more harmful of the two.

55. Has any one gained release from the cycle of subsequent births because the world was totally lost from view in his deep sleep or in the dissolution? The power of multiplicity can altogether bring about Liberation, but the thick veil of ignorance is the sole cause of the present calamity.

56. You may argue thus: Since the power of multiplicity is said to be a superimposition like the appearance of silver in mother-of-pearl and is therefore false, the Liberation gained by the aid of this false power must also be equally false. (The answer is:) A frightful dream, though unreal, ends in waking up the dreamer from sleep. Even so Liberation is real.

57. Just as poison is commonly antidoted with another poison, an iron spike is extracted with another (piece of) iron, arrows are turned aside by others, and dirt is washed away with other dirt, so ignorance which is weak in itself, can be eradicated by methods which are themselves of the same *maya*; later this also perishes like the wooden pole that is used to turn a burning corpse.

58. Through this *maya*, *jivas* experience seven stages of development as follows: ignorance,[19] veiling,[20] multiplicity,[21] indirect knowledge,[22] direct experience,[23] freedom from misery,[24] and supreme Bliss.[25]

---

[19] *avidya* [20] *avarana* [21] *vikshepa* [22] *paroksha jnana* [23] *aparoksha jnana* [24] *dukha nivritti* [25] *sukha avapti*.

59 & 60. Of these, ignorance is to lose sight of the fact that the inner self is no other than Brahman; veiling makes one say 'There is no Brahman. I do not see Him'; multiplicity springs up as 'I am a man. I am a *jiva*'; indirect knowledge is to know the nature of the Self, by the teachings of the Master; direct experience is to stay unshaken as the unitary Being after enquiry into the Self; freedom from misery is to end limitations and the sense of doership, and Supreme Bliss is the final accomplishment, *i.e.* release from bondage.

61. I shall now relate to you a story to illustrate this: Ten men forded a stream and, on reaching the other shore, each of them counted nine others and omitted to count himself. They were all perplexed (because the tenth man was missing).

62 & 63. Ignorance is want of right understanding and causes confusion. 'The tenth man is missing — not to be found' — this thought is the veiling. Grief at the loss of the companion is *vikshepa*. To heed the words of a sympathetic passer-by who says, 'The tenth man is among you', is indirect knowledge. When the kindly man further makes one of them count the others and points to the teller as the tenth man, the discovery of oneself as the missing tenth man forms direct experience. The cessation of grief for the lost man is freedom from misery. The joy of indubitable ascertainment by oneself is Supreme Bliss.

64. The disciple prayed: "Lord, Master! pray show me my real Self so that I may know It as truly as the tenth man did in the anecdote."

*Master:* "There is the *mahavakya* 'That thou art'. The verb 'art' in it establishes the identity of the pronouns 'That' and 'thou' in their ultimate meaning. I shall explain how it does so. Hear me.

65. Just as the ether though single is fourfold as the wide expanse, the ether in the clouds, the ether in the pot, and the reflection in water, so *chit* (Consciousness), which is single, is called the all-pervading Brahman, *Ishwara*, the Self, and the *jiva*.

66. In the *mahavakya* referred to, the word 'That' stands for almighty *Ishwara* and 'thou' stands for the *jiva*. But ultimately they both mean Brahman, who is free from *maya*, and the inner Self who is free from limitations. They are now mutually bound up like butter in boiled milk. Just as the milk is churned and the butter separated, so also you should realise the Self and thus stand apart.

67. The way to get rid of the trappings (of the *jiva*) is to kill the present idea that I am the body, which is only a corpse after all, for it is a mere assemblage of the five elements. Nor can you be the breath which moves through the nostrils like the blasts of air blown by bellows. It is simply a function of *rajoguna*.

68. Can the Self be the intellect or the mind which stand to each other in the relation of agent and instrument? These two sheaths are only modes of *sattvaguna*. Let not the unedifying bliss of deep sleep be mistaken for the Self, for it is only a mode of *tamoguna*.

69. Know 'thou', as the Self, to be *sat, chit, ananda*, the even, unchanging, single, eternal and all-pervading Witness and rid yourself of the trap of the five sheaths which are of an opposite nature — false, insentient, painful, etc."

70. *Disciple:* "When I dissociate myself from the five sheaths and look beyond, there remains only a blank. I see nothing more than that. Am I to take this blank for the supreme experience of the Self? Tell me this truly, my Master."

71. On this request of the disciple, the Master further said: "In the anecdote the tenth man, of deluded intellect, after counting only nine men and not recognising himself as the tenth, was stupefied. Can such stupor be the tenth man? Good son! you are the seer of all (the 'blank' and the 'five sheaths').

72. By the Lord under the sacred banyan tree! speak the truth: You are the unchanging Witness of the gross, subtle and (causal) ignorance, the waking, dream and sleep states, and the passage of time — past, present and future, which endlessly rise and fall, like waves in the ocean of bliss.

73. Do not ask 'By what light shall I see myself who am the all-seeing Witness?' Can there be a light to illumine the self-luminous Light? The tenth man knows himself as such among the others — Is there an eleventh man in him?

74. To argue that knowledge is necessary to make knowledge known, is foolish, and leads to interminable controversy. You are neither known nor unknown. Realise yourself as self-shining Knowledge.

75. Is it not because that the nature of sugar is to be sweet that makes the sweets sweet? Realise yourself as the meaning of 'I', which makes objects known as 'this' and 'that',[26] and Itself lies beyond them.

76. The Self, as described above, is the primary meaning of 'thou' (in the *mahavakya*: 'That thou art'). Brahman which is never bound by limitations is the primary meaning of 'that'. Their secondary meanings are the transient *jiva* and *Ishwara* respectively. Two separate entities can never be identical.

---

[26] Or; 'the seen' and 'the unseen'.

77. The distinctions between *Ishwara* and the *jiva* are due to their names, localities, artificial limitations, bodies and capacities. They are as far apart as the upper and the nether regions. Their identity is unthinkable with these associations.

78. When the conventional acceptance of terms appear inconsistent, the pandits of ancient lore bring out the true meanings by employing three methods of exegesis: disjunction, conjunction or the two combined.[27]

79. (l) 'The house on the Ganges';[28] (2) 'The black remained and the red fled';[29] and (3) 'This is that Devadatta,' are (respective) examples of the above. The apparent contradictions in several scriptural passages are eliminated by a judicious use of these three exegetical methods.

(Here only the last is applicable)

80. In the example: 'This is that Devadatta', the man who was seen in another place and on another occasion, and also known as Devadatta, is this man who is seen in this place and on this occasion. Although the time and place are different, a little consideration reveals the man to be the same.

81. Similarly, in the words 'That' and 'thou', their literal meanings excluded, the Consciousness-Principle is taken as Brahman and the Witness, whose unbroken identity is established by 'art', so that Brahman is the Self, and the Self is Brahman.

---

[27] *Jahat lakshana, ajahat lakshana and jahadajahat lakshana.*

[28] Meaning the house on the shore of the Ganges, not on the waters of the river.

[29] Meaning the black cows remained and the red horses fled.

82. The ether reflected in water in a pot, and in the clouds,[30] are both circumstantial and therefore unreal, whereas the space in the pot and the wide expanse are together one and the same. Similarly, all-pervading Brahman and the Witness in the individual being are together one and the same. You must experience it so that you may remain fixed in the realisation 'I am the Reality'."

83. On hearing this, the disciple, loyal to the instructions of the Master, discarded the five sheaths and the blank, realised the Self as 'I am Brahman', went beyond that and remained as Perfect Being.

84. At the glance of the Master who was Grace incarnate, the worthy disciple sank into the Ocean of Bliss and merged as the undivided Whole, as pure Consciousness free from body, organs and all else, with mind made perfect and he became the true Self, unaware while awake.

85. After the blessed disciple had remained in that state for a long time, his mind gently turned outward. Then he saw his glorious Master before him. His eyes were filled with tears of joy. He was full of love and fell at the feet of the Master. He rose up, came round the Master, and with folded hands spoke to him:

86. "Lord, you are the Reality remaining as my inmost Self, ruling me during all my countless incarnations! Glory to you who have put on an external form in order to instruct me! I do not see how I can repay your grace for having liberated me. Glory! Glory to your holy feet!"

---

[30] The ether is invisible. But the region in which the clouds are, is marked off in our vision. It is therefore said to be the ether reflected in the clouds.

87. The Master beamed on him as he spoke, drew him near and said very lovingly: "To stay fixed in the Self, without the three kinds of obstacles obstructing your experience, is the highest return you can render me."

88. "My Lord! Can such realisation as has transcended the dual perception of 'You' and 'I', and found the Self to be entire and all-pervading, fail me at any time?"

The Master replied: "The truth that I am Brahman is realised from the scriptures or by the Grace of the Master, but it cannot be firm in the face of obstructions.

89. Ignorance, uncertainty and wrong knowledge are obstacles resulting from long-standing habits in the innumerable incarnations of the past which cause trouble, and then the fruits of realisation slip away. Therefore root them out by hearing Truth, reasoning and meditation.[31]

90. Checked by incantations,[32] fire will not scorch. Likewise defective realisation will not put an end to bondage. Therefore devote yourself to hearing the Truth, reasoning and meditation and root out ignorance, uncertainty and wrong knowledge.

91. Ignorance veils the Truth that the Self is Brahman and shows forth multiplicity instead; uncertainty is the confusion resulting from lack of firm faith in the words of the Master; the illusion that the evanescent world is a reality and that the body is the self is wrong knowledge. So say the sages.

92. Hearing the Truth is to revert the mind repeatedly to the teaching: 'That thou art'. Reasoning is rational

---

[31] *sravana*, *manana* and *nididhyasana*.

[32] *Sthambhana*.

investigation of the meaning of the text, as already heard. Meditation is one-pointedness of mind.

If every day you do these, you will surely gain liberation.

93. The practice must be kept up so long as the sense of knower and knowledge persists. No effort is necessary thereafter. Remaining as pure, eternal Consciousness, untainted like the ether, and thus liberated while alive, one will live forever as *That* — after being disembodied also.

94. The wise, remaining like ether and liberated even here, are of four classes, namely *Brahmavid* (*i.e.*, knower of Brahman), *vara, varya*, and *varishta*, in order of merit.

95. The *Brahmavids* who by steadfast practice have gained clear realisation of Brahman, continue to perform even the hard duties[33] of their caste and stage in life, exactly as prescribed by the *shastras*, for the benefit of others, without themselves swerving from their supreme state.

96. Should passions rise up they disappear instantly and cannot taint the mind of the *Brahmavids*, who live in society detached like water on a lotus leaf. They look ignorant not showing forth their knowledge and remain mute owing to the intensity of inward Bliss.

97. *Prarabdha*, *i.e.* karma, which is now bearing fruit, differs in them according to the actions in past incarnations. Therefore, the present pursuits also differ among the *Jnanis*, who are all liberated. They may perform holy *tapas*; or engage in trade and commerce; or rule a kingdom; or wander about as mendicants.

---

[33] *varnasrama dharma.*

98. They would not think of the past or future; would partake of what comes unsolicited; would not wonder if the sun turned into the moon or at any marvel; whether the sky were to spread its shoots down like a banyan tree or a corpse were to be revived; nor would they distinguish good and bad, for they always remain as the unchanging Witness of all.

99. Among the other three classes, the *vara* and the *varya* remain settled in *samadhi*.

The *vara* feels concern for the maintenance of the body; the *varya* is reminded of it by others; the *varishta* never becomes aware of the body either by himself or through others.

100. Although there are distinguishing characteristics in the lives of the different sages, who are themselves very rare in the world, there is absolutely no difference in the experience of liberation.

What can be the use of the hard won *samadhi*?

The *Brahmavid* who is outwardly active, seems sometimes to feel the misery of calamities, whereas the others remain in unbroken Bliss.

101. Now if the *Brahmavids* live like the ignorant, how are they free from the cycle of births, and how is their ignorance gone?

The all-pervading ether remains untainted by anything; the other four elements are tainted by contact with objects. So it is with the *Brahmavid* and the ignorant

102 . The immortal *Vedas* declare that single-minded devotion to a holy sage is not only pleasing to Brahma, Vishnu and Shiva, but also secures the rewards of all the Vedic rites, and finally liberation from the cycle of births.

Now listen how liberation while alive persists after disembodiment also.

103. Manifold karma in store, gathered in many births, is altogether burnt away in the fire of *jnana*, like cotton in a huge conflagration.

Further accumulating karma can never approach the *Jnani*.

The karma which has brought about the present incarnation, is exhausted by experiencing its fruits.

104. How will the merits and demerits of actions during his experience of *prarabdha* cease to affect him later on? His detractors share the demerits, and his devotees the merits.

105. The causal body of ignorance is reduced to ashes in the fire of rare *jnana*; the visible gross body becomes a corpse in due course; then like a drop of water on red-hot iron, the subtle body is dissolved in the Self, which underlies these three bodies and remains absolute all along.

106. As soon as the entity of a pot is broken up the ether in the pot becomes indistinguishable from the all-pervading ether. So also when the limitation of the body is gone, the *jivanmukta* reverts to the natural eternal disembodied state of Liberation, free from beginning, middle or end, and in or out.

107. Just as the ether, though all-pervading, seems to be newly opened in a well which is newly dug, so Brahman, though ever-present, appears as if realised afresh by enquiry into the Self, as taught by a Master or the scriptures. Therefore, O son, be at peace. We are always the same limitless Being!

108. The whole universe is as unreal as water in a mirage, silver in mother-of-pearl, the city of *Gandharvas* in the air, the dreamland in a dream, the blue of the sky, the serpent in a rope, the offspring of a barren woman, the horn of a hare, or the thief in a thick post. O Son! Pure Consciousness is alone real. Do not therefore forget the Self at any moment."

Thus ends the First Section of *Kaivalya Navaneeta*.

SECTION II

# DOUBTS CLEARED AWAY

1. "Just as men dig a hole, gently plant a long post in it, fill it in with earth, ram it in to fix it firmly, so too I have taken to clearing away doubts, so that the realisation of the Self as the Supreme Consciousness may remain unshaken."

2. The disciple, pure minded and Self-realised, clung to his Master from the time of wrong identification of the self with the body to the moment of unmoded, unembodied liberation, like a young monkey to its mother.

3. Finding that the loving disciple was keeping to him like his shadow, the Master asked him: "Are you able to stay unshaken as a mere witness? Have all your doubts disappeared? Or, does the sense of differentiation creep in at times? Tell me your condition."

4. On hearing this the disciple bowed to the feet of the Master and said: "Father, dare the phantoms of differentiation, which can roam about only in the darkness of ignorance, in the wilderness of worldly life, appear to the inner vision in the broad daylight of wisdom, after the sun of your teaching has risen over the summit of your grace?

5. Even after the devil is exorcised, just as the person who was possessed is further protected by a talisman against any return of the trouble, so also though my ignorance has

already been dispelled by your teaching, yet, sir, I seek more from you that I may be firmly fixed in the Self.

6. You were pleased to say: 'Know it from the scriptures (that the Self is Brahman), the Non-dual Brahman cannot be reached by speech (study or discussion). It must be realised in the Heart. Self-shining Brahman cannot be reached by the miserable mind'. I have doubts about these two statements. Please clear them."

7. *Master:* "As Brahman is not an object of the senses nor of inference, and as there is no second to It, It is beyond direct perception, inference or analogy.[1] Also know that being free from attributes, It cannot be expressed by words.

8. The *Vedas* which declare that Brahman lies beyond words also signify It by the text ('That thou art'). If you ask which is right, know that both are right, for the *Vedas* can never be untrue.

9. A girl says 'Not he, 'Not he' of all others, and remains shy and silent when her lover is pointed out. In the same way, the *Vedas* clearly deny what is not Brahman, as 'Not this', 'Not this', and indicate Brahman by silence.

10. Having answered the first part of your question, I proceed to answer the second. The Heart governs the external senses, its faculties play, internally and externally, as intellect and mind.

11. As your face is seen reflected in a mirror, so the image of Pure Consciousness[2] is seen in intellect. Along with

---

[1] *pratyaksha, anumana and upamana.*

[2] *Chit-abhasa.*

this, mind proceeds to function, and this is called knowledge, my good son!

12. As molten metal takes the shapes of the mould into which it is poured, so the mind assumes the shapes of the objects, and they are revealed by the reflected light. Without eyesight and light, things in darkness cannot be discovered.[3]

13. The aid of a burning lamp and clear eyesight are required to discover an object in darkness. But to see the sun, eyesight alone will do. To see the manifest universe, both moded mind[4] and reflected consciousness are necessary. But to realise the Reality, moded mind eager for realisation will alone do.

14. The union of the moded mind and the reflected self is called the mind. Brahman can be reached by the mind for the reason that the mode of mind directed to itself is necessary for realisation. Brahman, cannot be reached by that part of the mind which is reflected consciousness. Thus reconciling the meaning, be free from doubt."

15. *Disciple:* "Worthy Master of unerring wisdom, I have understood your teaching so far. Please let me ask you another question: Free from movement, unbroken, perfect, and transformed into *That*, is not such a state of mind called *samadhi yoga* (or union in Peace)? How can this mind always moving like a swing, and raising up several worlds in a trice, be stilled so that it may remain steady in the Self like a flame protected from draughts? Tell me kindly."

---

[3] Light removes darkness but the object must be seen by the eye. Similarly the modes of mind are objects which are illumined by the reflected light of the mind.

[4] *Vritti.*

16. *Master:* "The active mind is composed of three *gunas*; when one of them is uppermost, the other two lie covert. With *sattvaguna*, divine qualities manifest; with *rajoguna*, the tendencies pertaining to the world, the body and the *shastras*.[5] With *tamoguna* the evil nature[6] manifests.

17. *Sattva* is the very nature of the mind, whereas the other two qualities are mere adjuncts and can therefore be banished from it.

If one holds steadily to one's divineness, *rajas* and *tamas* get strangled, so that the internal stresses and the external manifold disappear. When this happens, your mind shines forth untainted and becomes motionless and subtle like the ether. And then it naturally becomes one with Brahman, which is already so, and remains in undifferentiated Peace (*Nirvikalpa Samadhi*).

18. When one stainless mirror is placed in front of another similar one, the reflecting surfaces will be one undistinguishable whole. Similarly when the mind which is clear has become one with the Infinite, *sat-chit-ananda*, Brahman, and remains untainted, how can there be the manifold or movements in the mind? Tell me."

19. *Disciple:* "How then can the wise, liberated while alive, exhaust their *prarabdha* if their mind has lost itself in Brahman and become one with It? Is it not done only by experiencing its results? Such experience would certainly require the mind. There cannot be any kind of experience in the absence of the mind. If the mind persists, how can they be said to be liberated? I am confused on this point. Be

---

[5] *Loka vasana, deha vasana and sastra vasana.*

[6] *Asuri sampat.*

pleased to clear this doubt of mine, for I cannot be liberated unless all my doubts are cleared away."

20. *Master:* "The annihilation of the mind is of two grades: namely, of the mind pattern[7] and of the mind itself.[8] The former applies to sages liberated while alive; the latter to disembodied sages.

Elimination of *rajas* and *tamas,* leaving *sattva* alone, is the dissolution of the pattern of the mind. O sinless one! when *sattva* vanishes along with the subtle body, the mind itself is said to have perished too.

21. *Sattva* is pure and forms the very nature of the mind; when *rajas* and *tamas* (which give the pattern to it) are destroyed (by proper practice), the identity of the term 'mind' is lost. For, in such a state, the sages will partake of what comes unsolicited; not think of the past or future; nor exult in joy or lament in sorrow; getting over their doership, becoming non-doers; witnessing the mental modes and the three states[9] they can remain liberated while they pass through *prarabdha*. There is no contradiction in it. You need have no doubts on this point.

22. On hearing that the whole period of activity is also the state of peace, you may object, saying, 'Does not action denote changing mind, and on such change does not peace slip away?'

The state of the sage is like that of a girl who never ceases to thrill with love for her paramour, even while she attends to her duties at home."

---

[7] *Sarupa:* lit., *in its form.*

[8] *Arupa*: lit., (the mind) *which has no form.*

[9] The waking, dream and dreamless sleep states.

23. *Disciple:* "Should the sage, liberated while alive, who has transcended the incidents of the body,[10] lost the sense of doership and the whole individuality, and become one with Brahman, be said to be the experiencer of *prarabdha*, he must also be the doer. Can there be experience to a perfect non-doer? Master who removes all misery! please elucidate this point."

*Master:* "Hear their greatness as Perfect Doers, Perfect Enjoyers and Perfect Renouncers.

24. As a hill of lodestone neither moves of itself nor puts things in motion, and yet pieces of iron orient themselves towards it, I neither act by myself nor actuate others, and yet the whole world is active before me. Like the Sun I remain an unconcerned witness of all the functions of the body, senses, etc. and also of the state of Peace that results from merging the mind in Brahman. One possessed of this firm experience is the Perfect Doer.

25. The Perfect Enjoyer is he who partakes of anything that comes his way without discriminating whether it be tasty or not, clean or unclean, healthy or unhealthy, like a blazing fire consuming all that lies in its way. He whose mind is crystal clear, unaffected by passing phases, great or small, good or bad, his own or others', is the Perfect Renouncer. A liberated sage is strictly an exemplar of these three virtues (united)."

26. *Disciple:* "How can it be reckoned that the task of the sage is finished[11] if by *prarabdha* he lives on in a body acting and teaching to satisfy others desirous of liberation?

---

[10] The subtle and the gross bodies; caste, creed and so on.

[11] *Kritakritya.*

O Master who so graciously removed the cause of my misery! kindly answer me."

27. *Master:* "Occupations of people are of three kinds: Those pertaining to life, here or hereafter, are only for the ignorant, possessed by the desire for enjoyment,[12] sense of ownership[13] and attachment to the body. Only those who long for deliverance turn to the learning of the Truth, etc. Is there anything to be gained by learning or other similar actions for a person who is all-perfect?"

28. *Disciple:* "O crest jewel among Masters! hear me. It is right that they alone can practise true wisdom who have deliberately discarded the joys of life here and hereafter. Can those who have turned away from worldly activities and rituals to tread the path of liberation ever turn back to the old methods?

Are not hearing, reasoning and meditation necessary to make the mind firm? Tell me truly!"

29. *Master:* "Wise son, hear me. They who do not know must learn the Truth (as taught by the scriptures and Masters); those who have doubts must engage in reasoning; those who are in the grip of wrong knowledge must practise meditation. Can there be anything wanting for those who have become the real ethereal Being-Consciousness-Perfection?"

30. *Disciple:* "Lord, hear me! Can the wise also say like the ignorant, 'I did – I saw – I ate and I went'? You say that they are free from wrong knowledge. Can realisation of Brahman, which is real, admit of such expression? Please enlighten me on this point."

---

[12] *Bhogeccha*.

[13] *Mamata*.

31. *Master:* "A person who wakes up from a dream speaks of his experiences in the dream. In the same way, the Self-realised sage though using the language of the ignorant is not bound as the ego. A man who commits himself to the flames on the eve of his becoming an immortal god is spoken of only as a man, until his body is reduced to ashes. So also, the ego-free sage appears to function like others until he is disembodied."

32. *Disciple:* "If so, O Master! though the objects are unreal, would not the transactions (associated with them) cause misery? Can they bestow the bliss of knowledge? It can be felt only in their absence. Is it not necessary to be one-pointed? And if the person practises it, can he be said to have finished his task?"

33. *Master:* "Self-realised son! activities end when *prarabdha* ends. Is not practice of *samadhi* or worldly work an activity of the mind? Being one with the transcendent Self, can he do anything different from IT? Should he be practising *samadhi*[14] he cannot be said to be established in the Self."

34. *Disciple:* "Master supreme! how is it then that some of those who are established in the Self, and have nothing more to do, practise mind-restraining meditations?"

*Master:* "I have already told you that the sages, liberated while alive, appear to be active in many ways according to their *prarabdha*.

35. "My good boy, hear me further. The activities of the sage are solely for the uplift of the world. He does not stand to lose or gain anything. The Almighty who is only

[14] There are said to be six kinds of *samadhis*.

the store of grace for the world, is not affected by the merit or demerit of the creation, etc."

36. *Disciple:* "O Master, you who are formless (transcendentally), function as *Ishwara* (cosmically), and appear in human form (here)! You speak of a *Jnani* and *Ishwara* as the same. How can that be so?"

*Master:* "Yes. *Ishwara* and the *Jnani* are the same because they are free from "I" and "Mine." The *Jnani* is himself *Ishwara*, the totality of the *jivas*, and also the cosmos."

37. *Disciple:* "Lord, if as you say he is all *jivas* when he is liberated, how can others remain bound? If the *jivas* are said to be diverse, he cannot be all. All-knowing Master! please answer me this question in detail."

38 & 39. *Master:* "The Self, which shines forth as 'I-I' in all, is perfect and impartite. But *jivas* are as diverse as the limitations in the form of ego (make them). Look how the moon, who delights the world, is only one, whereas her reflected images are as many as there are ponds, pools, tanks, streams, cisterns and pitchers of water. Where one of them is destroyed, the image is no longer reflected, but is re-absorbed in its original, namely the moon. It cannot be so with the other reflected images. In the same manner, the *jiva* whose limitations are destroyed is withdrawn into its source, the Self; others not."

40. *Disciple:* "How can a *Jnani* be the same as *Ishwara*, who is Brahma, Vishnu, and Shiva, the Lords of creation, preservation, and destruction of the universe? They can divine the thoughts of others; know the past, present[15] and future, and are immanent in all. O Master of immense

---

[15] Even remote or hidden.

austerities! I do not find even a trace of these qualities in the *Jnani*."

41. *Master:* "The water in a tank, and a powerful light, help the whole village, whereas a pot of water and a table-lamp help only one family in a home. O son in the company of the wise! *Ishwara* and the *Jnani* do not differ in their *jnana*.[16] However, associated with the limitations of *maya*, they are spoken of as superior and inferior.

42. Like the kings and the *siddhas*[17] among men, the gods, such as Narayana, have some extraordinary powers like *anima,*[18] etc., because of their extraordinary antecedent austerities. Although men do not possess these powers and therefore appear less, yet from the standpoint of Brahman there is not the least difference between them.

---

[16] Wisdom, namely the realisation 'I am Brahman'.

[17] Adepts who have acquired the knowledge of everything past and future, remote or hidden can divine the thoughts of others, gain the strength of an elephant, the courage of a lion, and the swiftness of the wind, fly in the air, float on water, dive into the earth, contemplate all worlds at a glance, and perform other strange feats.

[18] The powers are eight:

1. *Anima:* Shrinking to a minute form.
2. *Mahima:* Enlargement to a gigantic size.
3. *Laghima:* Levitating (e.g., rising along a sunbeam to the solar orb).
4. *Prakamya:* Possessing unlimited reach of the organs (as touching the moon with the tip of a finger).
5. *Garima:* Irresistible will (for instance, sinking into the earth as easily as into water).
6. *Isita:* Dominion over all beings animate or inanimate.
7. *Vasita:* Faculty of changing the course of nature.
8. *Prapti:* Ability to accomplish everything desired.

43. *Disciple:* "O Master who has caused my deliverance! although there have been many sages in the world who possessed these extraordinary powers like *anima* (minuteness), etc., you say these powers are *Ishwara*'s own. Please make the matter clear to me."

*Master:* "Know that the powers are the fruits of their devotion to the Glorious Almighty Being, their austerities[19] and practices of Yoga."[20]

44. *Disciple:* "O Shiva in the form of my Master! If these powers and deliverance are together the fruits of *tapas*, then all the sages should possess both, as the ancient sages did. We have known that the ancient sages had these *siddhis* and were also liberated at the same time. Why do not all *Jnanis* possess such powers as well?"

45. *Master:* "Of the two types of *tapas*, namely, *tapas* for the fulfilment of one's desires[21] and dispassionate *tapas*,[22] the former bestows the powers desired, and the latter wisdom. Each can yield its allotted fruits only. That is the law. The ancient sages had evidently performed both kinds of *tapas*.

46. "Sinless son, Janaka, Mahabali, Bhagirata and others got deliverance only. Did they display any *siddhis*? (No). Some of the sages sought *siddhis* only; others sought both *siddhis* and emancipation. These *siddhis* are simply for display and nothing more. They do not make for liberation."

47. *Disciple:* "If emancipation be the sole outcome of the realisation of identity of the individual self with the universal

---

[19] e.g., fasting, prayers, rituals.

[20] Meditation with control of breath, in particular postures.

[21] *Sakamya*.

[22] *Nishkamya*.

Self, how then did some of the sages[23] who were liberated here and now, exert themselves for the attainment of *siddhis*?"

*Master:* "*Prarabdha* spends itself only after bestowing its fruits that are experienced (as pain or pleasure). Therefore the *siddhis* gained by emancipated sages must be considered to be the results of *prarabdha* only."

48 & 49. *Disciple:* "O Master who so graciously answers all my questions with holy texts and reasoning, so that my mind may remain unshaken. I am now free from the delusions of the mind[24] and remain pure and clear. There is certainly no harm in cleaning a mirror[25] a little more even though it is already clean.

O Lord who has removed my misery! Your words are like nectar and do not satiate. Can the scriptures say anything that is not absolutely true? Gracious Master, how can I reconcile the two statements: the karma of any person wears away only after bestowing its fruits; and the fire of pure wisdom burns away the karma which is waiting to bear fruits later on?"[26]

50. Master: "My son, the *jivas* are unlimited (in number, capacity and kind), and their actions also are similarly unlimited. In three sections, the beneficent Vedas prescribe[27] according to the aptitudes of seekers, with preliminary views

---

[23] e.g., *Chudala* (*vide Yoga Vasishta*).

[24] The delusions are of five kinds: (1) that the world is real, (2) that I am the body, (3) that I am the doer and the experiencer, (4) that I am separate from the Almighty, and (5) that Pure Consciousness is not "I" but *Shiva*.

[25] The ancient metallic mirror is meant here.

[26] *Sanchita Karma*.

[27] *Karma, upasana* and *jnana*.

succeeded by final conclusions,[28] like flowers followed by fruits.

51. Is it not true that sinners who must suffer in hells can yet be saved from them by means of pious gifts, *mantras*, austerities, *yajna* and the like? He who has faith in the saying of the *Vedas*, that the fire of *jnana* burns away all karma waiting to yield its results, attains Liberation."

52. *Disciple:* "Beloved Master who ever abides in the tabernacle of my heart! When true wisdom can root out the karma which has been accumulated in many incarnations, and liberate the person, why do even the most brilliant of men not profit by this wisdom, but fall into the rut of karma and perish? Please explain!"

53. *Master:* "My son, those of in-turned mind[29] will realise the everlasting *That*. Like absent-minded walkers falling into a ditch even with their eyes open, those of out-going mind look for the fulfilment of their desires, fall into the contemptible sea of never ending rebirths and cannot gain Liberation."

54. *Disciple:* "Are not the good and bad actions actuated by *Ishwara*? What can the *jivas* do who are themselves His creatures? How are they to blame, worthy Master?"

*Master:* "My son, hear me! These are words of illusion, worthy of fools ignorant of the clear meaning of the scriptures.

55. The creations of the Almighty Lord and of the individual *jiva* are different. The Almighty's creation is cosmic and consists of all that is mobile and immobile. The

---

[28] *Siddhanta.*

[29] *i.e.*, those who look on the diversity as an illusory phenomenon, or those who consider Brahman to be the undivided Whole.

unworthy *jiva's* creation, which consists of attachments, passions, desires and the like, pertains to the ego and is certainly not of the Almighty.

56. The creations of the Almighty Lord, who functions threefold,[30] may constitute the means for Liberation, whereas those of the *jivas* are the maladies which cause them successive reincarnations. Liability to birth does not end for anyone, even if creation comes to an end, but it ends on the giving up of one's passions and the like.

57. Whoever got free from rebirths at the time of the dissolution of the Lord's creation? (No one). Despite the persistence of time, space and bodies, people have been liberated even here, by destroying the illusion of individual creation, and gaining Knowledge. Therefore bondage and illusion are clearly of the *jiva's* own making and not of the Lord's.

58. There is a tree, called the Asvattha, and two birds live on it. One of them who is full of desires, enjoys the fruits, saying, 'This is sweet – this is sweet'. The other who is highly esteemed, does not eat thereof. Understand this parable by which the holy *Veda* describes the *jiva* and *Ishwara*.[31]

---

[30] As the Creator, Preserver and Destroyer.

[31] This parable is found in the *Mundakapanishad*. The body is compared to a tree because it can be felled. Its roots are high in the holy Brahman and its branches are low, as the vital airs and the like. Its duration cannot be definitely ascertained and therefore it is called *Asvattha* (*i.e.*, not dependable), the holy fig tree. Its stay is coeval with *ajnana* and therefore indeterminate. The *jivas* require the body for experiencing the results of their *karma*. Hence it is said to be the *kshetra* (abode). In this dwelling place, there live the two birds, namely the ego and the Universal Self who are respectively the experiencer and the unconcerned Witness.

59. Those fools head for disaster who in their ignorance attribute to God the six evils,[32] which are of their own making, but the wise will gain untainted deliverance who recognise the same evils to be of their own making and not God's."

60. *Disciple:* "O Master, who are Bliss incarnate! how is it that God who is impartial, advances a few and degrades others?"

*Master:* "He is like the father who encourages his sons who are in the right way, and frowns on the other sons who are in the wrong way. Know it to be mercy to punish the erring and turn them to be righteous.

61. O son, whose fetters of worldly life are broken! the celestial tree,[33] fire and water, protect those who seek them, by fulfilling their desires, keeping them warm and quenching their thirst. So also *Ishwara* is kind to His devotees and not so to others. Now think well and judge whose fault it is.

62. Now, my son! here is the vital point: Rebirths will be at an end for him who adopts with perseverance the way to Deliverance shown by God in the scriptures, follows the sages, gives up his evil propensities, discriminates the Real from the unreal, rejects the illusion born of ignorance and gains Wisdom (by realising the Self). Then and then only will rebirths be at an end for him. This is the Truth.

63. This wisdom can be gained by a long course of practice of unceasing enquiry into the Self."

*Disciple:* "What is this enquiry?"

---

[32] viz., *kama, krodha, lobha, moha, mada* and *matsarya* (lust, anger, greed, delusion, conceit and jealousy).

[33] *Kalpakarvriksha.*

*Master:* "Enquiry consists in pondering over the questions: Who is this 'I' in the body, including mind, senses, etc.? What is sentience? What is insentience? What is their combination called bondage? What is Release?"

64. *Disciple:* "The cumulative effect of all the meritorious actions of past births would confer *jnana* on us. What is the need for an enquiry into the Self?"

*Master:* "Hear me! The unselfish actions which were rendered unto God help to keep off impurities, and make the mind pure. The mind which has thus been purified begins to enquire into the Self, and gains Knowledge."

65. *Disciple:* "Holy Master! is it not possible for rituals and other powerful actions which confer devotion, dispassion, happiness in the other world, supernatural powers, steadfastness in austerities, success in yoga, meditation and a divine form, to give right knowledge which removes illusion? What need is there for enquiry also?"

66. *Master:* "Hear me, son; if you want to identify the persons in a masquerade, you set about to discover their nature, habits and traits which are now hidden. If on the other hand, you run about, jump, turn somersaults, climb posts, dance and fuss about, that will not help you to recognise them.

67. Likewise enquiry alone can lead to the knowledge revealed in the *Vedas*, which only point to Brahman indirectly. Knowledge of the Self cannot be gained by a study of the *Vedas*, feeding the hungry, performing austerities, repeating mantras, righteous conduct, sacrifices and what not."

68. *Disciple:* "O Master of crystal clear wisdom! the stain[34] on a shining mirror can be removed only by rubbing it. Or

---

[34] The mirror is metallic and the stain is verdigris.

has anyone made it stainless by knowledge only? Similarly the dirt of ignorance should be removed by karma. How can it be done away with by Knowledge which is only mental? Tell me."

69. *Master:* "Son! the stain on a (metallic) mirror is material and also natural to it. But the black is not natural to the crystal (quartz). It is only superimposed on it. Appropriate work is doubtless necessary to remove the stain on the mirror. But to know that the black is a superimposition on the crystal, the mind alone will succeed.[35]

70. Here also, non-being,[36] insentience and misery are all superimposed on Being-Consciousness-Bliss by (the play of) *maya*. They are neither natural nor real. The series of karma does not conflict with *avidya* (ignorance) though it is perishable; on the contrary, it nourishes it. *Jnana* (Realisation) is the fire which burns away karma and ignorance.

71. A man who has forgotten where he left his things in the house cannot recover them by weeping even for a hundred years. But he will get them only if he thinks the matter over and finds out. The Self is realised directly by knowledge which destroys forgetfulness (ignorance), the root-cause of all misery, but it cannot be realised by any amount of hard work, though extended over several aeons."[37]

72. *Disciple:* "Master! why should the *Veda*, which says that *jnana* is the sole means of Supreme Bliss, classify karma, in the *Karmakhanda*, as merit, sin and a mixture of the two, which

---

[35] The Master compares ignorance to the colour transmitted by a clear crystal behind which a coloured foil is set.

[36] *Sunya:* blank, void.

[37] *Yugas.*

make the doers reincarnate as celestial beings, animals (beasts, birds, trees, insects and so on) and human beings respectively, and further prescribe special duties for different castes and orders of men as conferring happiness when properly done?"

73. *Master:* "Like the coaxing of a loving mother concerned with the sickness of her child who has eaten earth, and offers it a tempting sweet in which a medicine is wrapped, the cheering statement of the *Vedas* 'Do your household duties — perform sacrifices — they are all good!' means something different. It is not understood by seekers of pleasures in heaven.

74. Look, it is only natural that pleasure-seekers eat what they get and embrace whom they can. Would the scriptures dictate what is after all natural to everyone? Do they not know so much? No one need order: 'Crow, be black! Fire, burn! Neem,[38] be bitter! Fleeting wind, blow!'

75. When the *Vedas* enjoin: 'If you desire fermented drinks and meat, have them by performing sacrifices; if you have sexual impulse, embrace your wife', the person is expected to desist from other ways of satisfying his desires. The *Vedas* aim at total renunciation only."

*Disciple:* "In that case, why should there be these commandments at all?"

*Master:* "They are only preliminary[39] and not final.[40]

76. Note that the *Vedas* which advise thus: 'Drink the fermented juice — eat the meat', say later on 'smell it'. Note also the commandment: 'Desire sexual union for the sake of

---

[38] Margosa, or *azadirachta indica.*

[39] *purvapaksha.*

[40] *siddhanta.*

a child'. Note again (the commandment): 'Give up this also (*i.e.* sacrifice, marriage, wealth and other possessions)'. Note further that complete renunciation is not a slur on a *sannyasin* or a *brahmachari*. Understand the scheme as a whole, give up any desire for action, and thus you will gain Beatitude."

77. *Disciple:* "O Master! granting that actions simply aid the ignorance which gives rise to the world, if knowledge be inimical to ignorance which brings about this diversity, how can such ignorance coexist with stainless Knowledge, like the spot in the moon, and effect these creations?"

78. *Master:* "O son! Consciousness which is Itself self-luminous has two aspects: pure Consciousness,[41] and modal consciousness.[42] The former manifests as the latter and they are not therefore exclusive of each other. You have known that pure Consciousness is not inimical to ignorance in deep sleep. Modal consciousness burns away ignorance, which rests on pure Consciousness."

79. *Disciple:* "How can *maya* which expands and contracts like a bellows, remain unaffected by pure Consciousness, but be burnt away by modal consciousness?"

*Master:* "See how the sun shines over the whole world and sustains it, yet it becomes fire under a lens and burns. So also, in *samadhi*, modal consciousness can burn away ignorance."

---

[41] *Svarupa jnana:* all-diffusive, static consciousness.

[42] *Vritti jnana:* directed or particularised consciousness. These two can be compared to the latent energy in fuel and burning fire which reduces it to ashes, or to an electric current which remains unmanifest in a live wire and the same current which manifests as light in the filament of a bulb.

80. *Disciple:* "Do not actions include all modes of mind, speech and body? Is not modal consciousness a function of the inner faculty? Then should we not say that action (a special mode of mind) destroys ignorance? Why is it marked off with the imposing title of Knowledge? Please explain to me this."

81. *Master:* "Modal consciousness is truly a mode of mind, but we have seen that the sons of the same mother fight among themselves.

Actions pertain to the doer, whereas Knowledge born of enquiry, does not pertain to the individual,[43] but pertains to the thing in itself.[44]

82. The injunctions may be done, may not be done or be done differently,[45] but Knowledge, which is paramount, cannot be so.

Meditation (as 'I am Brahman') is certainly different from Knowledge obtained by enquiry. To formulate one thing as another is forced yoga.[46] Direct knowledge[47] alone can be true. Do not be deceived by fanciful ideas.

83. Knowledge is the result of direct experience, whereas meditation is mere mental imagery of something heard. That which is heard from others will be wiped off

---

[43] *Purusha tantra.*

[44] *Vastu tantra.*

[45] Even the *nirguna Brahma dhyana* may be done as prescribed, maybe omitted or may be done at the sweet will of the person. It is not intrinsic to the man as *jnana* is to the thing in Itself.

[46] There are different kinds of *dhyana*. In one of them, the *Saligram* is meant to represent Vishnu, who is four armed, holding a conch, a discus, a club and a lotus. This *dhyana* is forced but yet effective.

[47] *i.e.*, gained by experience.

the memory, but not that which is experienced. Therefore that which is experienced is alone real, but not those things that are meditated on. Know that knowledge but not karma is the destroyer of ignorance at sight.

84. Do not doubt that unreal meditation can grant real final deliverance. Hear me! During meditation the image meditated upon by hearsay is not real, but when it materialises and is seen face to face, it becomes real.[48]

85. If you ask how unreal meditation leads to real and everlasting deliverance: Each one is reborn in accordance with the last thought of his previous life.[49] Persons are reborn in the forms they meditated upon. But should one meditate upon the Self in order to do away with any kind of rebirth, then one becomes the Self. This is sure and certain."

86. *Disciple:* "If those who meditate on attributeless (*i.e.* transcendental) Brahman[50] become That, O Master in human form! where is the need for enquiry or for knowledge?

*Master:* "Meditation upon Brahman is based on hearsay;[51] however, it becomes a fact of experience in due course. This experience is called the everlasting enquiry, knowledge or *jnana* (which destroys ignorance), or deliverance. This is the final conclusion."[52]

---

[48] It follows that the 'I am Brahman' of the contemplative stage is not real but the resulting *experience* 'I am Brahman' is real.

[49] Vide *Srimad Bhagavad Gita*, Ch. VIII.

[50] *Nirguna Brahman.*

[51] *Paroksha.*

[52] *Siddhanta.*

87. *Disciple:* "If modal consciousness[53] (after destroying ignorance) be left over in the all-perfect Self,[54] how can there be the experience of undivided being?"[55]

*Master:* "Just as cleaning-nut[56] powder carries down the impurities[57] in water, and settles down with them, so also modal consciousness destroys ignorance and perishes with it."

88. *Disciple:* "Well, what is the nature of the wise, liberated here and now?"

*Master:* "They are free from thoughts and therefore live happily, like an undisputed suzerain of the whole world, or like a baby. The ideas of bondage and release vanish for them altogether, so much so that they laugh at those who speak of such things. For, are they not to be laughed at, who say that a mosquito took in the ether and vomited it forth?

89. The son of a barren woman and the man seen in the post[58] wore flowers gathered in the sky, wrangled over the price of the silver in mother-of-pearl,[59] in the city of the Gandharvas,[60] armed themselves with the horns of

---

[53] *Vritti jnana.*

[54] *Paripurna.*

[55] *Akhanda anubhava siddhi.*

[56] *Strychnos potatorum.*

[57] Lit. 'the mud'.

[58] In dim light, a thick post is mistaken for a man. Such an illusory man is meant here. In a similar story the *Yoga Vasishta* mentions the reflected image of a man in a mirror.

[59] The nacre of mother-of-pearl is mistaken for silver. This fancied silver is meant.

[60] The Gandharvas are a class of celestial beings. At sunset, the clouds shine with gorgeous colours. In peculiar dispositions of such bright clouds, a fancy may sometime arise that it is the cheerful city of the happy Gandharvas.

hares,[61] fought and stabbed each other, died together and turned into ghosts.

No man of sense will be excited on hearing this story.[62]

90. Since *maya* itself is unreal, all its creation must likewise be unreal. Can the progeny be of a different species from the mother's?[63]

Therefore, do not heed heaven or hell, good or bad; but stay as the Self which is *sat-chit-ananda-purna* (Perfection)."

91. *Disciple:* "My Lord! tell me, is it not blasphemy to deny as unreal, the lotus-seated Creator and the other gods, the great men of the world, holy waters like the Ganges, the places of pilgrimage, the holy occasions, the four *Vedas* with their six auxiliaries,[64] the mantras and austerities?"

92. *Master:* "If it be sacrilege to deny dream-visions as false, it would be sacrilege too to deny the world[65] which derives its existence from illusion. If on the other hand it is right to deny dream-visions, it is only right to deny the world also which is derived from illusion.

93. If the *Puranas* hold up as men of merit the ignorant who regard the false as true, does any *shastra* attach censure to the *Jnani* for calling the truth, truth?

*Maya*, which appears as the elements and their modifications with different names and forms, is false. Only the Self which is all diffusive as *sat-chit-ananda*, is the Truth."

---

[61] They are non-existent.

[62] The story starts with two non-existent men and indulges in mere fancy. The world and its activities are no more real to the *jnani* than this story is to an average man.

[63] *e.g.*, can a mare bring forth a human being, an elephant or a bird?

[64] Such as *Chandas, kalpa, jyotisha.*

[65] With its contents.

94. *Disciple:* "O Master who are like a typhoon in dispersing the clouds of *maya*!

(a) Of what nature is *maya*?

(b) Who are in its grip?

(c) How did it come into being?

(d) Why did it arise?

(e) Duality is inevitable if *maya* is separate from Brahman.

(f) If not separate, Brahman Itself is false (like *maya*)."

95. *Master:*

(a) "Because its nature is not determinable, *maya* is said to be inexpressible.[66]

(b) They are in its grip who think: "This is mine — I am the body — the world is real."

(c) O Son, no one can ascertain how this mysterious illusion came into being.

(d) As to why it arose, it is because of the (person's) want of *vichara* (discerning enquiry).

96. (e) and (f): A magician's unseen powers remain unknown until hordes of illusory beings make their appearance in the show. Similarly the countless powers of Brahman remain unknown, but they are inferred only after the manifestation of the elements.

97. The magician who stands on *terra firma* and the hordes (conjured up by him) are visible to the onlookers. But his wonderful genius for magic remains mysterious. So also the handiwork of illusion (the world) and the wielder of the illusion (*i.e.* Brahman) are visible, but not the power of illusion. There are many powers distinct from Almighty Brahman and the world.

---

[66] *Anirvachaniya.*

98. The power is not apart from the wielder. The wielder of magic is real, but the apparitions (of magic) are not. Wise son, you can from this illustration ascertain the true nature of the Reality which is the wielder of illusion and which at the same time remains whole and as the Self. Thus, get clear (of your doubts)."

99. *Disciple:* "Why should the power which is unreal, be said to exist?"

*Master:* "Good-natured son! look how the grasses and their like which appear insentient, put forth blossoms and bear crops. But for the consciousness pervading them all, the mobile and immobile beings would lose their immemorial nature.

100. See the wonder, how the embryos in eggs develop into birds of so many hues! But for the governance of an unseen force, all (the laws of nature) would be blotted out, like a kingdom without a king. Fire would turn to water; a bitter thing taste sweet; even the degraded recite the *Vedas*; the immovable mountain ranges float like clouds in the air; all the oceans become sandy wastes and there would be no fixity anywhere."

101. *Disciple:* "O Master who are the transcendent Reality! how can this power of consciousness (*i.e. maya*) which cannot be seen or known or expressed by anyone in words, and forms the root-cause of diverse names and forms, be rooted out? Otherwise how is Brahman to be meditated upon as the non-dual Reality, to gain deliverance?"

102. *Master:* "What becomes of the well-known qualities of air, water or fire when they are checked by amulets or incantations? If you stay as *sat-chit-ananda*, free from other thoughts, *maya* becomes extinct. *No other method can be found in the whole range of the Vedas.*

103. What remains unmanifest in clay, becomes manifest (as a pot). For the practical purposes of life, the word makes earth a pot and destroys it. To discard names and forms and recognise the clay, is true knowledge. In the same manner discard the fancied notions of plurality of beings and realise the Self as pure Consciousness."

104. *Disciple:* "Though false, how can the persistent appearance of non-being — insentience — misery in the fullness of Being-Consciousness-Bliss be wiped away?"

*Master:* "Though the reflection in the water appears head downwards and tremulous, yet when the figure on the ground is considered, which remains upright and steady, that worthless image is only unreal.

105. Knowledge is the cause, and objects the effects. It is fruitless to discuss how the phantoms of names and forms came into being and how they will vanish.

Worthy son! not caring how this long-drawn out dream of the world came into being or how it is withdrawn, only remain aware as the Consciousness-Self which is all embracing.

106. To the degree that you turn away from attachments to the unreal, your inner vision of Reality develops. If by a steady practice of this kind, the mind comes under control and becomes aware as Consciousness-Self, you can abide as the ocean of Bliss though living in the bitter body."

107. *Disciple:* "O Master! I do not see the propriety of the statement that all beings are permeated by the single non-dual Self which is all-embracing as Being-Consciousness-Bliss. The existence of the *jivas* is clear because they all say 'I'; Consciousness also is clear because of knowledge which is obvious; why does not Bliss show forth in a similar way?"

108. *Master:* "Son, although there are shape, fragrance and softness together present in the same flower, each of them is cognised by a separate sense only. Otherwise they are not perceived; such is the law of nature. Similarly, though the beatific qualities, Being, Consciousness and Bliss together form the Self, yet the modes vary constantly and give rise to the differences which appear as the world.

109. My son! the three qualities — *sattva, rajas* and *tamas* — give rise to the three modes — repose, agitation and ignorance respectively. Being, Consciousness and Bliss which are themselves glorious, always remain a homogeneous whole, yet appear different.

110. Bare existence alone is noticed in plants, minerals and the earth, which look insentient and are ignorant.

There can be no happiness in the state of disturbance caused by passions, such as lust, which act like poison. But Being and Consciousness are evident in it.

Being, Consciousness and Bliss together become manifest in the state of Peace which is characterised by a stern detachment (from externalities).

Therefore Bliss becomes clear in a peaceful mind rid of ignorance and agitation."

111. *Disciple:* "Lord who has appeared as my Master in the world! I do not clearly understand the character of Being-Consciousness-Bliss (*sat-chit-ananda*). What is this *sat*? What is *chit*? And what is *ananda*?"

*Master:* "*Sat* (Being) is that which does not perish at any time — past, present or future.

*Chit* (Consciousness) is that which cognises the different objects.

*Ananda* (Bliss) is the joy arising out of the experience of bliss during the enjoyment of an object of desire."

112. *Disciple:* "O Master who like an elephant in rut, attacks and demolishes the forts of the sheaths,[67] although the *mahavakyas* in the four *Vedas* declare 'Thou art *Sat-Chit-Ananda*' to the indweller in the mortal body, and Masters say 'Thou art Brahman', yet how can one experience 'I am *Sat-Chit-Ananda*'?"

113. *Master:* "When it is said that rebirths are the inevitable results of past actions, does it not follow that the person was existent in the past? Again should heaven and hell be the rewards of present actions, does it not follow that he will continue to exist in the future? A subtle body (suited to heaven or hell), a celestial body, or a human body which are all the results of illusion, often change and pass away. Always surviving the false body, it is but right to say that he is *sat*.

114. In the darkness covering deep sleep and night, when there is no sun or lamp, he is unmistakably aware of darkness and objects, so he is *chit*.

He is also *ananda* because his love never fades for the incomparably beatific Self, for love manifests only for an object of pleasure.

115. Food, drink and so forth are dear to all alike because pleasure is derived from them. The Self is not likewise a means to beatitude. Should the Self described above be classed along with other means of pleasure, where is the pleasure apart or the enjoyer thereof? Can the Self be two?

116. Love for sensual pleasure is evident, but the love for the Self remains unrivalled. The love for sensual pleasures undergoes changes whereas the intense love for the Self remains unchanging. Sensual pleasures can be enjoyed or

---

[67] *Annamayakosa, etc.*

rejected, but who is there to accept or reject the Self? The Self can reject all other pleasures but not reject itself.

117. It is wrong to imagine that the Self kills itself and gets rid of itself by committing suicide in a burning passion. He who kills the body cannot be the body given up by him. The disgust is for the body and never for the Self.

118. Wealth is much sought after, but a son is dearer than wealth; one's own body is dearer than a son; the senses are dearer than the body; the life breath is dearer than the senses and the Self is very much dearer than life itself. This Self is the essence and the other three selves — the secondary[68] (viz. the son), the illusory[69] (the body) and the acting[70] ones (the ego) — successively increase in importance.

119. At the time of one's death, the secondary self, namely the son, who succeeds to the father's estate, assumes prominence. At the time of nourishment, the illusory self, namely the body, is prominent. When a happy future life is desired, the acting self, *i.e.*, the ego, becomes prominent. But in the state of Liberation, the Self, to wit pure Consciousness, is paramount.

120. Even a tiger becomes a favourite when it is obedient and a son is hated when he thwarts one. In this world, the things like straw which are neither loved nor hated, are treated with indifference. But under no circumstances does the love of the stainless Self diminish for anyone.

Therefore, my son, investigate your true nature which is unbroken Bliss only and realise the Self!"

---

[68] *Gauna atma.*

[69] *Mithya atma.*

[70] *Karta.*

121. *Disciple:* "Worshipful Master! How many kinds of *ananda* (bliss) are there?"

*Master:* "There are three:

(1) *Brahmananda* (which shines as pure Consciousness, e.g. in sleep);

(2) *Vasanananda* (which is present in reminiscence); and

(3) *Vishayananda* (which is the joy of gaining the desired object).

However others say that there are eight kinds of *ananda*. The above three cover the other five (of the eight). I shall nevertheless tell you all these eight. Hear me.

122. (1) *Vishaya sukha*[71] the pleasure of sensual enjoyment;

(2) *Brahma sukha:* the bliss of dreamless sleep;

(3) *Vasana sukha:* the remembrance of the above for a few minutes immediately after waking;

(4) *Atma sukha:* the happiness which ensues on determining that the Self is the dearest of all dear things;

(5) *Mukhya sukha:* the bliss of *samadhi* when the veil of ignorance is completely lifted;

(6) *Nija suhka:* the contentment which results from indifference;

(7) *Advitiya sukha:* the happiness of holding on to the Self to the exclusion of duality;

(8) *Vidya sukha:* the happiness that results from the enquiry into the Self in accordance with the scriptural texts.

---

[71] They are: (1) Objective delight, described later in v. 123; (2) Delight in Brahma, in vv. 124-127; (3) Reminiscent delight, in v. 128; (4) Delight in Self, in vv. 95-107 and 164-166; (5) Paramount delight, in v. 130; (6) Natural delight, in v. 129; (7) Non-dualist delight, in vv. 114-121 and 167; (8) Delight of Knowledge, at the end. *Sukha is ananda.*

123. My son! hear me describe their distinguishing characteristics. A man who is always exerting himself in the waking state, seeks rest on his bed, out of sheer exhaustion. Then his mind is well turned inwards and in that state it reflects the image of the bliss of Consciousness which shines by Itself. The pleasure which he then experiences, represents objective pleasure.[72]

124. The person who, feeling objective pleasures poor because they involve the painful triads,[73] keeps the mind in repose and falls into sleep, like an eagle dropping into its nest, becomes one with the limitless transcendent Being and remains as the blissful Self. This supreme state of Bliss is unrivalled *Brahmananda* [see v. 122-(2)].

125. That the bliss of deep sleep is *Brahmananda*, is the statement of the scriptures. That some persons take elaborate care to provide themselves with downy beds to sleep on, is the fact which supports it. That in that state, all sense of right and wrong, of man or woman, of in or out, is totally lost as at the time of the embrace of the beloved, is the experience which confirms it. So it is *Brahmananda*, sure and certain."

126. *Disciple:* "O Master, adored even by the gods! You are all-knowing and can kindly clear this doubt of mine: In this world of cause and effect, the experience of one cannot be felt by another. In deep sleep, the intellectual sheath has subsided and the blissful sheath has the experience of happiness. Is it right that this experience

---

[72] *Ananda* has already been said to be the characteristic of *sattva guna* which is the state of repose. Therefore any shade of *ananda* must be traced to the mind which is free from agitation, even sensual pleasure.

[73] The enjoyer, enjoyment and the object enjoyed.

should be remembered by the intellectual sheath which expresses it?"

127. *Master:* "Know that these two (stand to each other in the relationship of) melted ghee and solidified ghee. They differ in their (limiting) thoughts, but not in their (intrinsic) knowledge. The intellectual sheath limited by the mind and active in the waking state, and the blissful one made of the bliss of pure Consciousness which appears when the painful mind subsides in deep sleep, are not different from each other, just like rain-water and the water stored in a reservoir, or like sugar and syrup."

128. *Disciple:* "In that case, why should any one lose hold of that non-dual bliss of Brahman and come out of it?"

*Master:* "He is drawn out by the force of his past karma. The man who has just wakened from deep sleep does not immediately lose the happiness of sleep for he does not bestir himself at once nor forget the happiness. This short interval of peace which is neither sleep nor waking, is the bliss of remembrance [see v. 122 (3)].

129. At the instant the 'I-am-the-body' idea starts, he loses himself in the troubles of the world and forgets the bliss. His past karma brings on pain or pleasure. Peace results in equipoise. Everyone has experienced the state void of thoughts and the pleasure consequent upon it. This is *nijananda* [*see v. 122 (6)*].

130. Can this be the bliss of *samadhi*? (No). The external moisture is not the water contained within the pot. This happiness (of indifference) is only the shadow of the bliss of yogic *samadhi* cast upon the rising ego. When the ego subsides and *samadhi* results there is the state of 'Repose' in which the mind is not aware of the environments nor asleep, and the body stays stiff like a post.

131. Of the happiness enjoyed by the sole sovereign of the world, the earthly Gandharvas and celestial Gandharvas,[74] the brilliant *piris*,[75] the gods existing from creation, the later gods and celestial chiefs, Indra,[76] Brihaspati,[77] Prajapati (or Virat)[78] or Hiranyagarbha or (Brahma),[79] each is a hundred times as great as the preceding one. Yet all are fragmentary and like froth and foam in the waters of the Deluge of *Brahmananda*.

132. Whosoever remains in the *turiyatita*[80] state, the seventh[81] (and the highest) plane, his experience of Consciousness-Bliss is the same as that of Narada, Suka, Shiva, Vishnu, Brahma and such others, free from duality or sleep. May the dust of his holy feet settle on my (humble) head!

133. So far I have now told you of five kinds of *ananda*; I shall later describe the bliss of knowledge [*see v. 122 (8)*]; I have already described the bliss of the Self[82] as the dearest of all and the bliss of the non-dualist Self[83] while explaining

---

[74] A class of celestial beings who enjoy music, dancing, etc.

[75] The elders of the gods, because they were created before them.

[76] The king of the celestials.

[77] The preceptor of Indra.

[78] The Creator of the gross world.

[79] The root of the Creation.

[80] Lit., beyond the fourth. The waking, dream and sleep states are the three which have their basis in the Self, so it is called the fourth in relation to the other three. But when the Self is realised as the sole Reality comprising all, there is no duality and related things. It is therefore absolute.

[81] The spiritual planes are (1) *subheccha*, (2) *vichara*, (3) *tanumanasi*, (4) *sattvapatti*, (5) *asamsakti*, (6) *padarthabhavani*, and (7) *turiyaga* (the transcendental state which is beyond description).

[82] *Atmananda*.

[83] *Advitiyananda*.

*maya* and *sat-chit-ananda*. O Son free from the pairs of opposites! tell me, have you any more doubts?"

134. *Disciple:* "O Master that has created and preserves Lord Subrahmanya, myself and the whole cosmos, hear me!

If each of the terms, *sat, chit* and *ananda* of which you have spoken, has characteristics of its own, how can the mind which is already unsteady be fixed (on unity)? I do not see that they are different words with the same meaning. I pray you kindly show me how it is all an indivisible, homogeneous whole, like honey which is uniform though gathered (from different flowers) by the bees."

135. *Master:* "Is water tripartite because of its coldness, fluidity and whiteness (*i.e.*, transparency)? Or is fire tripartite because of its light, heat and redness?

The *Vedas* have analysed and dismissed the cosmos, beginning with the ether, as unsubstantial, insentient and misery-laden. In contradistinction to this and for easy understanding they have described Brahman as *sat-chit-ananda*[84] which is One only.

136. The *Vedas* describe Brahman in affirmative terms as follows: the Eternal, Whole, Unique, the highest Truth, the Supreme Brahman, the Repository, or the Source, Peace, Ever-True, Absolute (continuum of the Source, dream and sleep states, and therefore) the Fourth, Continuous or Equal in all, the Sight, the Witness of all, Knowledge, Pure, (That which is) indirectly denoted (by the *Vedas*), Everlasting, Indweller, the Reality, Ether, Light, the Self, Liberation, the Lord, Subtle, and so on;

---

[84] Being-Consciousness-Bliss.

137. In negative terms as: the Unmoving, Untainted, Immortal, Immeasurable, Unsullied, (That which is) beyond speech, not insentient, the Diseaseless, Uncontaminated, Incomparable, Uninterrupted, Unattainable (by the mind or the senses), Undivided, Unborn, Infinite, Indestructible (That which is) without qualities, Undivided, without limbs or parts, Beginningless, Bodiless, Changeless, Non-dual, and so on.

138. When all these qualities, affirmative or otherwise, are considered together in the right way, they point to *One* only and there can be no other. Many may be the words to signify the same. Thus Brahman, signified by *Sat*, *Chit* and *Ananda* is One only. Realise this unity and remain as one undivided Whole.

139. Do not say: 'To describe Brahman by qualities is like speaking of a barren mother'. Can there be any one so talented as to understand the nature of Brahman without being told? What the *Vedas* have revealed out of grace for gaining knowledge of Brahman and liberation in life, are not qualities of Brahman but Brahman Itself."[85]

140. *Disciple:* "O Lord! Like millions of suns rising simultaneously, you have come forth as my Master to dispel the darkness of my ignorance! Hear me again.

In accordance with the statement of the *srutis*, I have now understood beyond doubt that my Self is the indivisible Reality. If you will further establish it by arguments, the truth will be fixed in my mind like an iron spike driven into a living tree."

---

[85] *Truth* is ascertained by three kinds of proofs, *shruti*, *yukti* and *anubhava*. Of these *shruti* is dealt with in vv. 130-139, *yukti* from vv. 140-143, and *anubhava* in v. 144.

141. *Master:* "*Being* must itself be *consciousness*. Should the *consciousness* be different from *being*, it must be non-existent. How then can the *being* be revealed?

Again, *consciousness* must itself be the *being*. If different from consciousness, it must be insentient. The insentient cannot exist by itself. Thus *being* and *consciousness*, being identical, it is also *bliss*. This is the most agreeable argument (lit., 'seminal line of reasoning'). Otherwise bliss will be non-existent and insentient and there can be no experience of *bliss* (which is absurd).

142. How is *sat* which exists at all times revealed? By itself or by another?[86]

*A:* By another.

*Q:* Is that other non-existent or existent?

*A:* Non-existent.

*Q:* Fool! Can the son of a barren woman effect anything?[87]

*A:* Then let it be something existing but different from the original *sat*.

*Q:* How is its existence revealed? You must[88] say; 'by another'. Will there be an end to this chain of existent things and their cognisers? Your answer is therefore untenable, so get rid of this false reasoning.

143. Listen to experience agreeable to scripture and reason. Since the bliss of profound sleep persists as memory, this bliss itself must be knowledge. There was nothing besides it. Existing in the dissolution and deep sleep, you witness the darkness of ignorance. Now entering the Heart abide as the all-perfect Self!"

* * * * *

---

[86] The Master frames the questions and answers himself.

[87] It is as absurd as the statement 'I am the son of a barren woman'.

[88] In conformity with your previous answer.

144. In accordance with the teachings of the Master who had himself realised the very essence of the several scriptures, this disciple too realised that Being, Consciousness and Bliss are but the same Reality, which is homogeneous like the honey that is gathered from different sources, and was long fixed in *samadhi*. When he opened his eyes he realised himself to be the screen on which moves the kaleidoscopic picture composed of the mobile and immobile objects of the universe.

145. *Disciple:* "O worthy Master after my own heart! is there anything more for us to do than to have this unique experience? To think and speak of it and to remain soaked with the experience, appears to be the only duty for sages. Be gracious to make clear to me how the previously mentioned (see v. 132) *turiyatita* or seventh plane of knowledge is the highest."

146. *Master:* "After analysis, the elders say that there are seven stages of ignorance[89] and seven degrees of knowledge.[90] Of them all, first hear me mention the seven states of ignorance. The elders have named them thus:

1. *Bija-jagrat:* the germinal state of waking
2. *Jagrat:* the waking state
3. *Maha jagrat:* the waking state firmly established
4. *Jagrat-svapna:* the state of daydreaming (castles in the air)
5. *Svapna:* the dream state
6. *Svapna-jagrat:* cogitation of the dream after waking up from it, and
7. *Sushupti:* dreamless sleep.

---

[89] *Ajnana saptabhumi.*

[90] *Jnana saptabhumi.*

147 & 148.

1. The germinal waking state is the uncompounded consciousness which rises up fresh from the unitary state of being.

2. The waking state contains the sprout of the ego which was previously absent from the germinal state.

3. The sprout of the 'I' and 'mine', which rises up with every birth, is the firm[91] waking state.

4. The fussy ego conjuring up visions is the dreaming-wakeful state.

5. To have uncontrolled visions while sleeping after a full meal, is the state of dream.

6. To be thinking of the dreams after waking up from them, is the waking-dream.

7. The dense darkness of ignorance is the state of deep slumber.

These are the seven states of ignorance. I shall now tell you the seven stages of knowledge which bestow Liberation.

149. The elders have analysed them as:

1. *Subheccha:* desire for Truth

2. *Vicharana:* investigation into the Truth

3. *Tanumanasi:* pure and attenuated mind

4. *Sattvapatti:* the Realisation of the Truth

5. *Asamsakti:* a detached outlook on the universe and its contents

6. *Padarthabhavani:* untainted awareness of Self

7. *Turiya:* the highest and indescribable state.

150 & 151.

1. To wean from unedifying associations and desire, to knowledge of the Supreme, is the first plane called *subheccha*.

---

[91] Firm because it shows itself as often as it rises.

2. To associate with enlightened sages, learn from them and reflect on the Truth, is called investigation.

3. To be free from desires by meditating on the Truth with faith, is the attenuation of the mind.

4. The shining forth of the highest knowledge in the mind, owing to the development of the foregoing conditions, is Realisation.

5. To be free from illusion by firm realisation of Truth, is the detached outlook on the universe.

6. The bliss of the non-dual Self, devoid of triads,[92] is untainted awareness of Self.

7. Sublime *Silence* of the very nature of Self, is *Turiya*. Hear why this seventh plane (v. 149) was said to be *turiyatita* (*i.e.*, beyond the *turiya*).

152. The first three planes are said to be *jagrat* (*i.e.*, the waking state) because the world is perceived (in them as ever before).

The fourth plane corresponds to *dream* (because the world is recognised to be dreamlike).

Even the dim perception of the world gradually vanishes and therefore the fifth plane is called the *sleep* state.

Transcendental Bliss prevails in the sixth which is therefore called *turiya* (*i.e.*, the fourth state relatively to the foregoing waking, dream and sleep states).

The plane beyond all imagination is the seventh one which the *Vedas* indicate as sublime Silence! (*i.e.*, *turiyatita*).

153. Some sages consider the name *turiya*[93] to be in conflict with the foregoing explanation of *turiyatita* which,

---

[92] Namely, the subject, the object and their link, *i.e.*, the cognisor, the cognised and cognition.

[93] The fourth.

according to them, will be the glorious Liberation after disembodiment.[94] In such a scheme, the sixth plane is the state of very deep slumber as compared with the dreamless sleep of the fifth plane.

I shall further tell you the peculiarities of these glorious planes.

154. Those who yet remain in the first three planes are practisers and not emancipated.

*Brahmavids* are those who have gone into the fourth plane; they are pure and liberated.

Those in the next three planes are respectively *vara*, *varya*, and *varishta*, *i.e.*, the eminent, the more eminent and the most eminent among the knowers of Brahman. I shall still further tell you the excellence of the planes of the enlightened.

155. Those who have remained in the first three planes and died before they reached the fourth plane, go to the happy regions; then they reincarnate and gradually gain Liberation. Surely they do not go to the unedifying lower planes.

O son! the first plane itself is difficult to gain. This gained, Liberation is as good as gained.

156. If they gain the first or second planes of enlightenment in this world, even *mlecchas*[95] are as good as emancipated. By the holy feet of my Master, this is true! Cursed be they that deny it! Doubt not the *Vedas*, common to all. Strictly following the indicated way, clearly realise 'I am Brahman'!"

---

[94] Videha mukti.

[95] The *mlecchas* are those who deprecate the *Vedas*.

157. *Disciple:* "O Lord who has taken me like rice out of paddy that is liable to sprout again! You have just said that the planes of knowledge lead even contemptible *mlecchas* to final Liberation. But some say that Liberation cannot be gained unless the person renounces all domestic ties and retires as a *sannyasin*.[96] Please clear my confusion on this point."

158. *Master:* "Son worthy of respect by the righteous! Your doubt is right; hear me clear it. The renunciation which snaps domestic ties is of four kinds. They are: (1) *Kuteechaka*, (2) *Bahoodaka*, (3) *Hamsa* and (4) *Paramahamsa*, all of which are a panacea to the miseries of the world. But detachment and not the habiliments (ochre robes) is the sole requisite for such renunciation.

159. Detachment is again of three degrees according as it is dull, intense and very intense. That which is caused by a shock, is impulsive and dull. Discarding home and wealth for good is the intense form. Disgust for *Brahmaloka* as being illusory is the very intense.

160 & 161. Dull detachment does not qualify one for *sannyas*.[97] Intense detachment makes the person eligible for the first two orders of *sannyas*. If strong and fit he must move about as a *bahoodaka*; otherwise he must stay (at one place) as a *kuteechaka*.

---

[96] Here is the implication: *sannyas* is the fourth stage of life for a *brahmin*. He starts as a *brahmachari* and learns the *Vedas*, then marries and becomes a *grihasta*; then retires as a *vanaprastha*, and lastly renounces everything and becomes a *sannyasin*. Some say that the *kshatriyas* are also eligible for *sannyas*, e.g., Raghu. Others say that the *vaisyas* too can take *sannyas*, but not the *sudras* and the rest.

[97] Because shock is the result of past sins, whereas *sannyas* is the fruit of virtue.

When detachment is very intense, he can take to the *hamsa* or *paramahamsa* order. They say that the *hamsa* cannot gain final liberation unless through *satyaloka,*[98] whereas the *paramahamsa* can gain it here and now.

The *paramahamsa* order which is so efficient, is again of two grades.

162. A *paramahamsa* may be one who desires to know the Truth or is a realised being. The former is an intelligent practiser in the first three planes. The latter is a remarkable and pure sage who is liberated here and now.

The former class of *paramahamsa* is of two kinds. Here me speak of them also.

163. Of these, one will give up the ties of home (according to ritual), formally enter the order of *sannyas* and gain Supreme Knowledge.The other kind remaining as brahmins, *kshatriyas, vaisyas* and *sudras*, gains Supreme Knowledge.

Knowing it from the *shastras* and in actual practice, why do you still get confused? You must clear yourself by the authority of the *srutis*, your own reasoning and immediate experience.

164. If birth be a fact, then death is inevitable. But I am Brahman who is never born. If I be that which is born, this 'I' cannot surely be Brahman. Therefore I am that 'I' which is birthless and deathless Brahman."

165 & 166.

*Q.* "If I am Brahman, how does it happen that I do not know this 'I'?"

*A.* "Who says 'I' now?"

*Q.* "The intellect."

---

[98] *i.e.*, *Brahmaloka* to which he goes after death.

*A.* "The intellect gets lost in a swoon. That which remains is never lost, as perfect Consciousness is 'I'."

*Q.* "This state of perfection is not clear to me. How can I experience it?"

*A.* "There is the experience of happiness in deep sleep, and it is *That*. No happiness can be experienced anywhere when a want is felt. Therefore the Self must be this perfection. This is the source of all.

167. The cosmos originated in the imagination of the mind. Reason shows that these worlds have their being in that Consciousness. If the enquiry is pursued into the self as transcending all this and extending limitless, 'I' remains as the one perfect Being."

168. *Disciple:* "How should I remain so that I may experience what you have described as Bliss?"

*Master:* "If you get rid of that mode of mind which gives rise to the states of waking, dream and sleep, you will remain as your true being and also experience Bliss.

169. If you ask how to control the activities of the mind, rising up from its latencies: rule over the intellect and senses as your slaves. They will become extinct.

170. Also by gentle control of the breath which blows like a bellows, the activities of the mind cease. If you are not inclined to practice this yoga, they will cease if you root out the massive ignorance of the causal body. Then too the mind stops its activities."

171. *Disciple:* "By what means can I root out ignorance, the causal body?"

*Master:* "The *srutis* can never mislead one. How can there be ignorance if you firmly fix their teaching in your mind: 'I am the all-perfect being in whom the worlds appear'?"

172. *Disciple:* "How can I remain so when I engage in worldly transactions, with the mind wandering?"

*Master:* "There is nothing apart from Me. Whatever is seen, is of Me. I am the 'I' who is consciousness, which sees all this as fictitious as my dream.

173. If you always remain aware that 'I' am perfect Consciousness, what does it matter how much you think, or what you do? All this is unreal like dream visions after waking. I am all-Bliss!"

174-177. *Disciple:* "I had in my countless past incarnations mistaken the body for the self. High or low, seeing all as a mirage, I have by the grace of my Master realised the Self as 'I' and have been liberated.

What meritorious work have I done? I cannot describe my good fortune. I am blessed by the grace of my Master, Narayana, of Nannilam! In my ecstasy I throw my cloth in the air, and dance for joy!

How noble have my parents been that they named me Tandava (Dancer), as if they even then foresaw that I would be overpowered by the joy of having realised the Self and therefore dance in ecstasy!

Before whom shall I pour forth this ecstatic Bliss of mine! It rises from within, surges up, fills the whole universe and floods unbounded!

I bow to the lotus feet of the Almighty who was so gracious as to bring me into contact with a Master who could teach me the Truth according to the holy texts!

*  *  *  *  *

178 & 179. Such is *vidyananda*. Those who study this work with devotion will realise the high state of repose and be liberated here and now. In order that all may clearly understand *vidyananda*, the true spirit of the Holy books, in Nannilam, Master Narayana appeared in my *samadhi* and commanded me to make this *Kaivalya Navaneeta,* perfect in every detail and free from defect.

180. Through the Grace of his Lord, Tandavesa has shown how, freeing oneself from everything interior and exterior, one may be transformed into the ONE; and having been convinced that the intended sense of the *Vedas*, which are beyond thought, is 'I', and that the body and such are but modes of Sound (*nada*), one may become the 'All Eye' and see everything as oneself.

181. Those who, without wavering, recognise the One Witness of blazing lustre — *turiyatita,* which is perfected in the meaning of those three most excellent words: 'That thou art' — will unravel the knot of 'differences' and overcoming every obstacle, will be themselves absorbed in the SELF.

182. This is the "delight of knowledge" spoken of by the *Vedas*. Those who worship the feet of Narayana, who has described it, are without blemish; those who, through the teacher of this pupil, approach the stage in which doubt is finished and steadily go forward to Perfection, will obtain spotless Emancipation.

183. The author has, through the two parts of this work, kindled the sublime light of the spirit, so that the eternal darkness of *maya* may perish and, clearing all doubts rising from mental knowledge, which is affected by differences, has subjected the disciple to himself.

184. Praise, praise to the author of my salvation! He placed on his head the foot of Narayana, the Infinite Lord, who had made him his slave, and who, by means of the process of negation has destroyed what through imposition had arisen as a mere fictitious appearance, and put me in such a condition that I, with eyes of grace, can remain for ever the Spectator.

185. Just as the refreshing, cool water from the holy feet of one's wise Master sprinkled on one's head confers all the merits obtained from all the holy places of pilgrimage, so also the learners of this unique work acquire the merits of all the holy books and live as sages in the world.

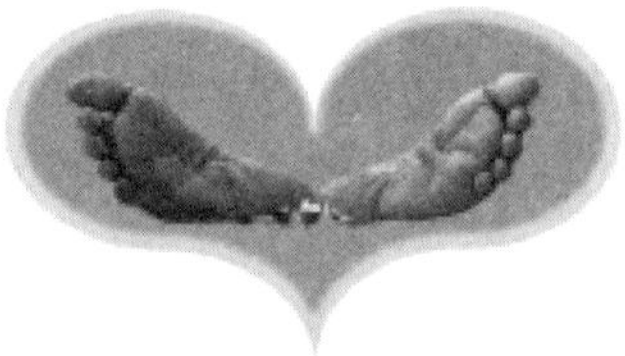

**OM TAT SAT**

**SRI RAMANARPANAMASTU**

# APPENDIX I

| *No.* | *The planes of Enlightenment* | *I Scheme* | *Remarks* | *II Scheme* *Remarks* |
|---|---|---|---|---|
| I<br>II<br>III | *Subheccha*<br>*Vicharana*<br>*Tanu-Manasi* | *Jagrat* (the waking state) among the *Jnana-bhumikas* | Because the world is perceived in them as ever before | |
| IV | *Sattvapatti* | *Svapna* (dream) | Because the Reality underlying the world is realised and the world itself appears like a phantom. | |
| V | *Asamsakti* | *Sushupti* (sleep) | The darkness of ignorance is totally lost and therefore it corresponds to sleep in the planes of enlightenment. | |
| VI | *Padartha bhavani* | Dense *Sushupti* | There is no place for the cognisor, the cognised and cognition.<br>The person cannot himself wake up from this state unless external influences draw him out forcibly. | *Turiya*. Because it is fourth in relation to three previous states. |
| VII | *Turiya* | Sublime Silence | Existence as the Self only, whether manifest or unmanifest. | *Turiyatita*. That which is beyond the *Turiya*. |
| VIII | *Turiyatita* | *Videha Mukti* | The state of Liberation after disembodiment. | Not taken into account because there is nothing to speak of. |

# APPENDIX II

| *Brahmachari* | *Grihasta* | *Vanaprasta* | *Sannyasin* |
|---|---|---|---|
| who is a bachelor and learns the *Vedas* | who marries and becomes a householder. He performs the rituals as *Yajna*, *Yoga*, etc. | who retires as a recluse for meditation and *tapas*. | who has renounced the world, and devotes himself to the spiritual quest and realisation. |

| (1) *Kuteechaka* | (2) *Bahoodaka* | (3) *Hamsa* | (4) *Paramahamsa* |
|---|---|---|---|
| He is physically weak and therefore stays in some chosen place. However, he is engaged in the quest of Truth. | He is strong and able to visit the holy places He always moves about, all along keeping his spiritual quest in view. | He goes to *Satyaloka* after disembodiment from this world and there gains liberation. | |

*Paramahamsa*:

- *Jijnasu*, *i.e.*, one who is desirous of knowing the Truth.
  - a formal *sannyasi* who observes rituals. He is always a brahmin only.
  - an informal *sannyasi* who is however highly developed, and therefore does not care for rituals and formality. He may be of any caste, or even a *mleccha*.
- or a *Jnani*, *i.e.*, a realised sage. He is liberated here and now.

(1) & (2) These two orders are for persons who are detached from the ties of home. Their detachment is of the middling quality.

(3) & (4) These two orders of *sannyas* are only for them whose detachment is of the nobblest kind, *i.e.*, ingrained and true. They do not care for anything but the Truth.